# The Wisdom & Laughter

## Laughter

of

## Leslie Jordan

I0541927

**The Wisdom & Laughter**
**of**
**Leslie Jordan**

*The publisher's profits will be donated to LGBTQ+ organizations.*

business@knightsbridgepublishing.com

ISBN: 978-1-998847-00-6

The quotations included in this book have been gathered
via multiple digital sources and researched for
authenticity and accuracy. Some
quotes collected are being presented without
context, and may therefore be imperfectly worded or attributed.
To the subject and original sources, our thanks, and where
appropriate, our apologies. – The Editor

Printed in the United States of America & United Kingdom

"

I fell out of the womb and
landed in my mother's high heels.

"

My mother had found this album
of all these old slides from the '50s
of me as a kid and I said, 'We should
have these made into pictures
because the color's so beautiful.'
There were pictures of me from 1955
as a little baby wearing all these
elaborate outfits, and in these pictures
was this amazing story of a gay man
and his mother.

"

I had 20,000 followers and I treasured
that. People'd say, 'Oh that's nothing.'
I said, 'What are you crazy? That's
20,000 people that wanna hear
what I gotta say!'

"

I remember stepping off and thinking that it might not be a good idea to let anyone know that I'm a homosexual, which is hilarious because I'm probably the gayest man I know. I had these huge dreams and they came to fruition so quickly.

"

I honor the sanctity of all religions
- I'm not here to put them down.
But the only religion that I personally
embrace is the religion of kindness.

"

That's the secret to happiness.
Find something you can make
money at that you really love to do.

"

I will never be a Robert De Niro
or Meryl Streep, the kind of actor
that disappears into a role.

"

I can tell when I meet you,
within three minutes, how
you were raised. When I met
Lady Gaga on the 'American
Horror' set... beautifully brought up.

"

Well, hello fellow hunkerdowners.

"

What amazes me with 'Will & Grace' fans is how young they are and how straight they are. The guys always come up and go, 'You are so funny on that show. My girlfriend watches that show.'

"

I grew up in the Baptist church and,
honey, they baptized me about 14 times.
It never did take.

"

I'd do an exercise video because there are so many gay men with these perfect abs and they do exercise videos. So I did an exercise video where my stomach looked like my water's about to break.

"

I knew I was as gay as a goose.
Then I ended up in West Hollywood,
where the queers hang from the
trees. I was home. I had landed.

"

In a perfect world we'd want gay
people to play gay people, but I
think that's a good rule of thumb:
Whoever gives the best audition should
get the part. My problem is getting
anybody to hire me for anything
other than queens.

"

There are two or three ways
to combat homophobia - one
is through humor. The second
is to put a face on it.

"

There isn't a lot I can do
on this planet, but I can
be funny.

"

I've always sang a little like a
16-year-old girl, but even
Ann-Margret stopped after
a while and brought it down a bit.

"

I've always been interested
in forensics and the way they
solve things.

"

When I hit Hollywood, it was full-blown. I was a party boy. It amazes me that I made it ... to be able to have led this amazing career when I was out every night. Every once in a while I'll see old reruns of myself and I see I'm giving it my comedy best, but with dead eyes - no sparkle. I was in the middle of all that abuse. But now I'm a recovering alcoholic with many years of sobriety.

"

For years, I had a Christmas ornament
I had bought at a Cracker Barrel that
read 'Deck Them Halls, Y'all.' It always
tickled me.

"

I talk about things that happened in my life. Now, do I embellish? Absolutely. Come on, we all do it. It makes for a better story. But it always comes from a germ of truth.

"

The thing that I love about 'Will & Grace' is that there's a clear-cut reason for my character to be there. I come in with the zinger. My character seldom has much to do with moving the story ahead. I know exactly what my job is there. It's just a party, basically. I'm just having a ball.

**"**

In the 1980s we had the huge catastrophe of AIDS and you would walk down the street and see someone who was dying. It was horrendous.

"

My sister was cute, she said,
'Oh my gosh, you're an overnight
success.' 'Oh,' I said, 'this is the
longest night.' I've been at it
since 1982.

"

I always call my journey into sobriety,
my journey into queerdom, because
I really did hate everything about myself.

"

People are really surprised when
they meet me that I'm a recluse.
People think I'm very gregarious
and outgoing - and I am - I'm thinking
about writing a book about it called
'The Gregarious Recluse.' How the
more that you put me out there in
front of audiences, the more that
when I have down time I have to disappear.

"

I'm Southern, I'm gay,
I'm little - I get Ma'am'd
a lot on the phone.

"

You know, you learned that very young in American culture that the feminine boys don't do well. And yet, I had a dad who was a lieutenant colonel in the army. My dad was a man's man, but he still adored me. And somehow in the midst of that, I still grew up hating the sissy in me.

"

In my day there was no one
to tell me anything and I feel
I have a responsibility to help
a new generation. A lady in
Atlanta came up to me and
said: 'Honey, you are a ministry.'
It is about the knowledge I can give others.
I think gays will look after their own.

"

From my years on
'Will & Grace,' you'd
think I'm Madonna.

"

I always thought I'd be good at
musicals, and it turns out I make
up for my lack of skill with enthusiasm.

"

When I was writing the book,
I thought "Who wants to hear
another story about some actor
who lost his way?" But my story
is a little unique in that I realized
when I was 14 years old that I
was different. I think a lot of gay
people use drugs and alcohol to
quell that fear and shame - especially
people of my age.

"

I have a lot of shame, and until
I got sober at 42 years of age,
I had never voted. I was just
a hippie.

"

I don't mind playing gay because
there's a whole plethora of gay
roles out there, but if I get asked
to play one more Southern hairdresser,
I'm going to scream.

"

People are realizing that being gay is just as defining as the color of our skin and it's not a choice. I'm really encouraged. I think in my lifetime we will achieve equality. I'm honored to be a part of it.

"

My mother and grandmother created
this secret garden where it was OK
for boys to play with dolls, and it
was OK for little boys to sew potholders.

**"**

People say, 'Oh, you do theater!'
And I say, 'Honey, I do theater to
get better TV and film roles.'

"

The only thing I know
how to do is be funny
- that's it.

"

I'm a true Hollywood success story - knew no one, had no connections.

"

Honey, I conquered Netflix.
I watched 'em all.

"

I love my family dearly.

"

There are many paths to God. What really bothers me - and what I think is the height of arrogance and stupidity - is when one group believes their way is the only way. That really gets my dander up.

"

I don't know why all three,
my comedic idols are... women.

"

We figured out as a community of gay people, we have to take care of our own.

"

I am not a drag queen.

"

I can spot a homosexual
at forty paces.

"

Time has taught me that
parents do the best they
can with the light they are
seeing with. That is what we
all do.

"

I can entertain myself for hours.

"

Well shit, what are y'all doing?

"

I'm one of the most popular cabaret performers, and I don't sing a note. And nobody expects me to sing.

"

In my head I have had the most torrid affairs with actors I have worked with. You should hear what George Clooney and I have got up to!

"

We've got to be kind.

"

Beverley Leslie was closeted. I'm not closeted. He was a little homophobic. He's a social climber. I'm nothing like that. He had a mean streak. I don't think I'm mean at all.

"

'Big Brother' has put me off people. I thought, 'I'm gonna get a dog.' I really think I'm going to become more reclusive. It was nothing like I expected. I was so naive about it.

"

Lesbian humor is nothing like gay men's humor. We're sillier.

"

I had 20,000 followers and I treasured
that. People'd say, 'Oh that's nothing.'
I said, 'What are you crazy? That's
20,000 people that wanna hear
what I gotta say!'

**"**

# All my life I've always been so ashamed of being feminine

"

I had a degree from the University of Tennessee at Chattanooga, where they said, 'Mr. Jordan, please learn to pronounce your degree.' 'Cause I said I have a degree in 'thee-a-ter'.

# Knightsbridge Publishing Group